INSIDE...

Published 2018.
Little Brother Books, Ground Floor, 23 Southernhay East, Exeter, Devon, EX1 1QL
Printed in Poland.
books@littlebrotherbooks.co.uk | www.littlebrotherbooks.co.uk

The Little Brother Books trademarks, logos, email and website addresses and the GamesWarrior logo and imprint are sole and exclusive properties of Little Brother Books Limited.

LittleBrother BOOKS

KT-155-788

A HISTORY OF FUN!

How a short teaser trailer from the 2011 SpikeTV Video Game transformed into one of the most **successful video games of all time!**

Ask anybody what Fortnite is and they will be able to tell you, it's that big of a deal; in fact it's probably the biggest deal ever in the world of video games. Everybody is playing it, including celebrities, parents, and kids of all ages; heck we've even seen YouTube videos filled with grandparents playing the game for the first time.

It's a cultural phenomenon like no other, and it all began with that first trailer revealed to the world all the way back in 2011 at the SpikeTV Video Game Awards presented by actor Zachary Levi, star of the upcoming DC Comics live-action movie, Shazam! The awards ceremony is one of the most popular events in the gaming world's calendar, and with then Design Director Cliff Bleszinski in attendance that night fans of Epic Games titles such as Gears of War and Bulletstorm knew they were in for a special treat.

THE BIG REVEAL

"We've had amazing success with games like Gears of War and Infinity Blade this year, but we decided it was time to switch things up a little bit and do something different and fun," said Bleszinski during the live broadcast that millions of gamers around the world tuned into. "Imagine a world where you explore, you scavenge, you build and ultimately you survive." As the lights went down and the trailer began to unspool the world was introduced to Fortnite for the first time.

The game looked very different from what Epic had worked on in the past, particularly in terms of its art style, but fans of the studio were excited at the possibility of what lay ahead when the game was finally released to the world.

HAPPY BIRTHDAY!

How Epic celebrated Fortnite's first birthday.

With the game celebrating its first year on consoles and home computers Epic decided to run a limited time in-game event. There were numerous fun things to do including dealing damage to opponents to get the Fortnite Birthday! Emoticon, dancing at birthday cakes around the map to nab the Happy Birthday! Spray, playing 14 matches to unlock 5,000XP and finishing all three challenges for new Back Bling. Oh, and the Battle Bus was decorated with tonnes of balloons to mark the celebration!

Unfortunately it would be a whopping six years before that day came. The game originally started out life at a Game Jam held in Epic's headquarters, an event where developers gather to build and design a game in a super-short amount of time.

It wasn't one of the titles that came out of the fun session, but the team got to talking about slicing up elements of different genres and blending them together during the event, which would ultimately lead to the creation of Fortnite Save The World as a concept. It borrowed elements from Epics' own games, as well as the smash-hit building title Minecraft and zombie shooter, Left 4 Dead.

SHIFTING FOCUS

The game was very similar to the Save The World mode we know today, focusing heavily on harvesting materials, crafting forts and strongholds and battling hordes of monsters in a world gone

to hell in a hand basket. However, after that initial reveal development slowed to a crawl due to a number of contributing factors.

Firstly, the team wanted to shift focus to building the game in Unreal Engine 4 rather than Unreal Engine 3, which wound up taking a lot of time. Then the release date was pushed back in November 2013, and after this the team announced to the world that it would actually be

arriving as a PC exclusive free-to-play title in 2014. Sadly, that 2014 date didn't quite happen the way the developers had planned, because the only way you could get your hands on it back then was through an invite to the Closed Alpha test in December of 2014.

Bizarrely, the game then disappeared without a trace and two years later in 2016 it was revealed to the world that

development on Fortnite had been put on hold so that Epic could focus solely on the crafting of another game, a free-to-play multiplayer online battle arena shooter called Paragon. Much to the dismay of Epic, Paragon never made it out of Early Access despite being released in that state on PC and PlayStation 4 in March of 2016.

BACK TO BUSINESS

At one time Paragon had a huge seven million player base, but those numbers began dropping fast over time, ultimately forcing the team to make the tough decision to shut things down in April 2018 so that the studio could focus solely on putting everything it had into

Fortnite, which had become a worldwide hit with far superior player numbers and earnings.

Despite this unfortunate situation Epic did something very interesting with Paragon, it released $12 million worth of character models, weapons, sound effects and game assets for free to any developer using the Unreal Engine. Even with the game failing to officially launch, the content created by the team could now be put to good use by other developers beavering away on their own titles.

Finally, in July 2017 Fortnite Save The World was released to the world on PC, PlayStation 4 and Xbox One as a paid Early Access game, pulling in over one million players by August. The game

looked very different in terms of art style from what was originally announced, the reason for this being the team felt the original art design was too depressing and would irk players. They then went back to the drawing board and pulled inspiration from the likes of Pixar for the new look that has become so synonymous with the title we know and love today.

GOING MOBILE

Fortnite Battle Royale comes to phones and tablets!

In March 2018 Epic announced that the game would be arriving on mobile devices, and would feature the same gameplay, map and weekly updates that were being wheeled out to console and PC owners. The launch was incredibly successful for the developer with Battle Royale pulling in an astonishing $100 million in revenue in just 90 days. That makes it the third most successful mobile launch ever in terms of coinage behind Clash Royale and Pokémon Go.

BATTLE ROYALE ARRIVES

Right around the same time as the launch of Fortnite Save The World a game called PlayerUnknown's Battlegrounds was taking the world by storm, selling over five million copies in the first three months of release. Epic stood up and took notice of this, even going as far as directly referencing PUBG when it announced on its blog that Fortnite would be getting a Battle Royale mode. The add-on was whipped up in just two months, and released for free in September 2017 on PC, PlayStation 4 and Xbox One all at the same time.

Fortnite Battle Royale was a monstrous success, and by January of 2018 the game had amassed a whopping 45 million players thanks to an update that wove in new locations to the map. Couple this with the huge interest from gamers watching streamers such as Tyle 'Ninja' Blevins, who would later go on to team up with the musician Drake and set a new record for a Twitch streamer when his numbers hit 635,000 during that monumental match.

The game became so popular that even Marvel got in on the action by teaming up with Epic to bring Thanos to the game to celebrate the release of Avengers: Infinity War. The success of the game has even had an impact on real-world events such as football and rugby matches when Antoine Griezmann performed the Take The L dance when he scored against Croatia in the World Cup final.

THE FUTURE OF FORTNITE

Nobody quite knows what the future holds for Fortnite outside of the development team, but one thing's for certain – it's very bright! The team has done an amazing job of constantly evolving the game with new updates that flip the world on its head. The number of players keep rising too, and there are always cool costumes being added all the time, as well as countless weekly events that keep gamers engaged.

Frankly, we are astonished at just how good Epic has become at keeping the game feeling fresh throughout each of the seasons so far. One thing is for certain, we will be playing it for years to come and we're pretty certain you will too, because we suspect Epic has so much more to show us as the game evolves and transforms over time. Catch you on the battlefield, Fortnite fans!

EPIC LISTENS!

How Epic Games listen to its vast community of fans.

COLLECT THE SET!
TOMATOHEAD

Outfit

Extra saucey.
Part of the Pizza Pit set.

1,500

PURCHASE

The developer is extremely interactive with Fortnite players, so much so there have been suggestions from fans on social media that have eventually made it into the game in some form or another. Haunted Hills began life as a fan concept by a user on Reddit called Blorfie. Another Reddit user called Tursuboi, who posted a drawing to the site, inspired the Tomatohead skin from Season 3. Other additions suggest by fans included multiple emote wheels, friendly traps and map zooming.

FORTNITE ON PLAYSTATION 4

Your **one-stop** guide to Fortnite on Sony's flagship console.

Fortnite is arguably one of the most popular games on PlayStation 4 thanks to a hugely dedicated fan base, so if you're playing on Sony's flagship console, or thinking about upgrading to a PlayStation 4 Pro you're going to want to check out our guide, which covers everything from Cross-Platform Play to exclusive skins!

BATTLE ROYALE OR SAVE THE WORLD?

Fortnite on PlayStation 4 comes in two different flavours – you can either go for the completely free version, Fortnite Battle Royale, or pay for the full experience, which includes the PvE mode Save The World. There are two versions of the full game on the PlayStation Store right now. At the time of writing, the **Standard Founders Pack** will set you back £32.99, whereas the Deluxe edition of the game will cost you £49.99.

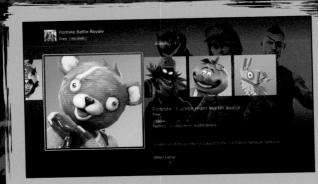

PLAYSTATION AVATARS

If you want to spice up your PlayStation Profile there are loads of Fortnite-themed Avatars up for grabs on the PlayStation Store, and the best part about these is that every single one of them are free. Yes, free! There's a whole bunch to choose from, including Llamas, the Leviathan, Jonesy, Rex and Tricera.

WINGMAN STARTER PACK

If you're just starting out on Fortnite Battle Royale and don't feel like spending huge sums of cash on the Battle Pass, additional skins and flashy combat gear, then this Starter Pack is an ideal first buy. At the time of going to press £3.99 will net you a slick **Wingman Outfit**, the Bogey Back Bling and 600 V-Bucks to spend.

EXCLUSIVE HEROES

If you buy the Standard Founders Pack or Deluxe Founders Pack you're treated to four exclusive heroes all clad in their PlayStation colours. This includes a Ninja, Outlander, Soldier and Constructor. To unlock the heroes all you have to do is just play the game and they will all become available over a short period of time.

PLAYING ON PRO

While Fortnite on a standard PlayStation 4 still looks great, if you're one of the lucky owners of the super powered **PlayStation 4 Pro** you are in for a real treat. The game renders at a native 1080p, scene lighting gets a massive boost and visual effects are bumped up to whole new levels of eye-watering brilliance.

PLAYSTATION PLUS GOODIES

If you're a PlayStation Plus subscriber then you are in for a treat with this exclusive and stylish skin for Fortnite Battle Royale. The PlayStation Plus Celebration Pack 2 features the Blue Striker Outfit and the Blur Shift Back Bling. It's really easy to download too, just search for Fortnite in the PlayStation Store and voila!

CROSS-PLATFORM PLAY

The PS4 version of Fortnite supports Cross-Platform Play with players on PC, Mac and the mobile version of the game. It also supports **cross-progression across all of these platforms**, which means you can link your Epic Games account to your PlayStation account and keep your progress and rewards no matter where you decide to play.

FORTNITE ON XBOX

Everything you need to know about playing Fortnite on the Xbox.

If you're the proud owner of an Xbox One console, or better an Xbox One X, arguably the most powerful games machine on the planet then here's everything you need to know about picking up a copy of Fortnite on Microsoft's games machine, including costs, essential peripherals, Xbox Live requirements, Cross-Platform Play and in-game items exclusive to the platform.

HOW MUCH DOES IT COST?

Fortnite Battle Royale is completely free on the Xbox Games Store, but if you want the full experience, which includes the Save The World game mode it's going to cost you. At the time of writing, the Fortnite - Standard Founders Pack costs £34.99 and includes a number of **exclusive items,** as well as the Battle Royale mode. The Deluxe Founders Pack includes all this plus a whole lot more and costs £49.99.

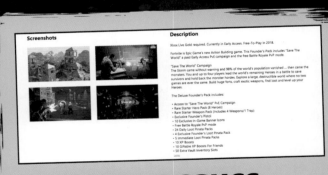

EXCLUSIVE STUFF

The Xbox version of the game also includes some pretty slick exclusive goodies for the Save The World mode, including Xbox Live inspired characters: Commando Renegade (Soldier), Guardian Knox (Constructor), Jade Assassin Sarah (Ninja), and Trailblazer Jess (Outlander). Just remember, if you want access to these characters you're going to have access to the Founders Pack.

12

ESSENTIAL PERIPHERALS

Now that you've picked up your copy of Fortnite on Xbox there are some essential peripherals you might want to consider to get the most out of the game. The first of these is a high quality headset for providing audio emersion to ensure pinpoint accuracy, and the second is the Xbox Elite controller, which features magnetic sticks, rubber grips and an improved D-pad.

DOWNLOADING FORTNITE

Downloading Fortnite on Xbox One is extremely easy: power up your console, navigate to the Xbox Game Store and use the Search Bar to find the game if it's not showing up on the page. Click on Fortnite Battle Royale if you want the free version or choose from one of the two Founders Pack if you want the full game.

CROSS-PLATFORM PLAY

Xbox One players can Crossplay with players on PC, Mac, mobile and Nintendo Switch but not PlayStation 4. To Crossplay with other players make sure you link your **Epic Games account** with your Xbox Live account and then add friends you want to compete with via the Epic Friends menu on the main menu of the game.

FORTNITE IN 4K

If you're lucky enough to own an Xbox One X and a 4K TV then you'll be happy to know Fortnite on Xbox includes full **4K resolution** at 60 FPS (Frames Per Second) and looks gorgeous. If you enjoy sharing your finest moments in the game with friends on social media you can be sure the footage is going to look amazing!

XBOX LIVE SUBSCRIPTION

Even though Fortnite's Battle Royale mode is free-to-play you'll still need an Xbox Live Gold account to in order to play the game online. If you've bought the full game, which includes the Save The World mode then you will need an Xbox Live Gold account to play that too. Xbox Live Gold accounts cost £39.99 for one year, at the time of writing.

Microsoft

XBOX LIVE

GOLD

12 Months

Play with friends online, and get free games plus exclusive discounts, on Xbox One and Xbox 360.*

DIGITAL CODE

FORTNITE ON NINTENDO SWITCH

Everything you need to know about Fortnite on Nintendo's handheld console!

Fortnite Battle Royale was unveiled - and launched just a few hours later - for the Nintendo Switch at the Nintendo E3 2018 conference. If you've been playing Fortnite Battle Royale on another console or desktop computer and feel like making the move to Nintendo Switch there are a few things you need to know before doing so.

NO SAVE THE WORLD

Fortnite on Nintendo Switch only includes the Battle Royale mode, which is still **free-to-play** and lets you spend real-world cash in the game store to purchase the Battle Pass and other items. It does not feature the **Save The World** mode, and as of writing Epic Games has said there are no plans to include it in the game.

NINTENDO SWITCH ONLINE

To play Fortnite Battle Royale you need a **constant Internet connection**, much like every other online-based game. However, up until recently you could play games online for free on Nintendo Switch, but as of September 2018 you're now required to have a Nintendo Switch **Online account** to play Fortnite Battle Royale.

GRAPHICS & FRAME RATE

The Nintendo Switch isn't as powerful as a PlayStation 4, Xbox One or PC, so that means the graphics in Fortnite Battle Royale have taken a slight hit, with resolution being a tad lower and pop-up more frequent when playing the Switch in docked mode. Moving to handheld mode means these things are less noticeable.

PRO CONTROLLER RULES!

You can play Fortnite Battle Royale just fine using the Nintendo Switch's **Joy-Cons**, but if you really want to get the most out of the control setup then we'd recommend using the **Pro Controller** if you already have one. If not, don't forget to pop one on your Christmas list to get the jump on your friends using Joy-Cons!

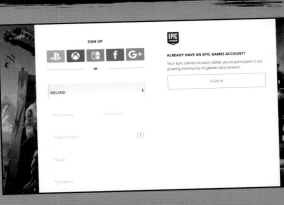

PLAYSTATION 4 PLAYERS

If you're playing Fortnite Battle Royale on PlayStation 4 and feel like making the move to Nintendo Switch you're going to have to set up a **brand new account** for the game. Sony currently doesn't allow Crossplay between consoles, which has been a massive pain for fans of the game who have decided to switch platforms.

V-BUCKS

Word of warning: if you had whole bunch of **V-Bucks** ed to your account on another console or esktop games machines they won't be ansferable across systems. However, **skins** nd **cosmetic items** you purchased can be sed across different platforms. It's annoying ut the fact is V-Bucks are tied to your ystem's account details.

CROSS-PLATFORM PLAY

Like other versions of the game Fortnite Battle Royale on Nintendo Switch is Cross-Platform, meaning you can face-off against other players on **PC, Mac, Xbox One** and **mobile devices**. Unfortunately you can't compete against **PlayStation 4** owners just yet, but Sony has said it is looking at the issue and hopes to come up with a solution for fans of the game sometime in the future.

FORTNITE ON DESKTOP

Everything you need to know about playing Fortnite on a PC or Mac.

Playing Fortnite on a desktop can be more expensive than playing on a console, not because there are more fees involved to enjoy the game, but because desktop and gaming rigs can sometimes cost a hefty amount of cash. It's possible to build one on a budget, but if you want a machine with all the bells and whistles then you had better be prepared to pay a hefty sum of cash for it.

PC SYSTEM REQUIREMENTS

Recommended PC Requirements
Operating System: Windows 7/8/10 64-bit
Processor: Core i5 2.8 Ghz
Memory: 8GB RAM
Video Card: Nvidia GTX 660 or AMD Radeon HD7870 equivalent DX11 GPU
Video Memory: 2GB VRAM

Minimum PC Requirements
Operating System:
Windows 7/8/10 64-bit
Processor:
Core i3 2.4 Ghz
Memory:
4GB RAM
Video Card:
Intel HD 4000

MAC SYSTEM REQUIREMENTS

Mac Requirements
Operating System:
Mac OS X Sierra
Processor:
Core i3 2.4 Ghz
Memory:
4GB RAM
Video Card:
Intel HD 4000

Note: *It's unlikely that Fortnite will run on your machine if you're using Yosemite or El Capitan. Your Mac must also support Metal API, which can be checked on the official Apple website.*

KEYBOARD & MOUSE

PC and Mac players will tell you that playing games such as Fortnite on a desktop or gaming laptop is better with a keyboard and mouse, especially when it comes to faster reaction times in crazy skirmishes on the battlefield. If you're serious about competing against others in the desktop version then invest in a good mouse and keyboard.

PLAYING WITH A CONTROLLER

If playing with a keyboard and mouse isn't your thing then don't fret. Fortnite on PC and Mac features controller support for both **Xbox** and **PlayStation 4** controllers. Setting up a console controller for Fortnite on desktop takes a little fiddling about, so be sure to do your research before plugging in and playing.

DOWNLOADING FORTNITE

Fortnite on PC and Mac isn't available on the widely popular game store Steam, and must be downloaded directly from the official **Epic Games' website** where you'll need to set up an Epic Games account that requires an active email address and password. Once you've done that you're all set to start playing the game!

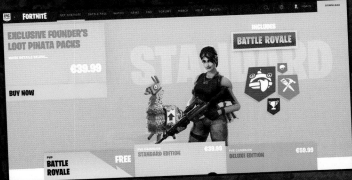

NO ONLINE SUBSCRIPTION

Unlike playing on an Xbox or Nintendo Switch you don't need to subscribe to any online services. All you need to be able to play Fortnite is an Internet connection. That means the only additional expenditure you'll need to cover is buying Battle Passes, in-game items, V-Bucks or upgrading to the Save The World PvE mode.

BATTLE PASS

Season 4 starts with a BANG! The more you play, the more rewards you unlock. Level up faster by completing Weekly Challenges to unlock additional rewards like progressive outfits, sprays and exclusive cosmetics.

BUY IN-GAME FOR 950 V-BUCKS

CROSS-PLATFORM PLAY

Fortnite Battle on desktop supports Cross-Platform play with **Mac, Xbox One, PlayStation 4, Nintendo Switch** and **mobile devices**, which means you can compete against players on every single platform the game is available on unless you're playing Solo Mode where it will match you with **PC** players only.

BATTLE ROYALE

STARTER GUIDE

Everything you need to know about getting started in the wild world of Fortnite Battle Royale!

What is Fortnite Battle Royale?

Fortnite Battle Royale is a free-to-play game developed and published by the team at Epic Games. It was released to the world on September 26th 2017, and is available to play on PlayStation 4, Xbox One, Nintendo Switch, desktop and mobile devices.

How Much Does It Cost?

The game will cost you nothing to download from the game stores on consoles, or from Epic Games' website if you're playing on desktop, but there are In-App Purchases, which means you can spend real-world money to buy things like new characters and gear.

100v100

The basic gameplay of Fortnite Battle Royale is simple: one hundred players are thrown onto an island and forced to duke it out in a frenetic duel to the end, and as the number of players remaining on the map dwindle the tougher it gets. (Note: this is just Battle Royale Mode, no 2 week timescale).

Solo Mode

Fortnite Battle Royale's Solo Mode is the ultimate endurance test for players who think they've got what it takes to compete in a gruelling battle to the end against a sea of other players all vying for that coveted top spot at the end of a single match.

Duo Mode

Duo Mode lets you team up with either another player from around the world or a friend. The goal is to work together to defeat the other Duos roaming the map, while looting, building and avoiding the ferocious Storm Circle closing in on you.

Squad Mode

Squad Mode is arguably the most popular of all modes. It lets you team up with up to three of your friends or a squad of random players, and the best thing is it allows you to have three sets of eyes watching your back on the battlefield at all times.

50v50 Mode

This Limited Time mode provides the perfect opportunity for fresh-faced Fortnite players to practice both building and combat skills by dropping two teams of 50 on opposite sides of the map. Building skills are pivotal to winning matches in Battle Royale and 50v50 is the perfect place to hone those abilities at the outset.

Spawn Island

Once you've chosen a gameplay mode you'll have to spend a bit of time waiting on the Spawn Island until the game fills up with 100 players. Once it has it's off to the main island to brawl, but while you're waiting you can play around with the controls, pick up weapons or do a spot of building.

The Battle Bus

The Battle Bus is what transports players to the main island at the outset of a match. However, you won't be getting there by roads, instead you'll travel to the island in the air thanks to a hot air balloon attached to the top of the blue bus.

Skydiving

Once everyone's inside the Battle Bus the rickety blue bucket of rust soars high over the waters towards the main island. As soon as it is over the ground below you can leap out the rear doors and skydive to a location of your choice using the glider.

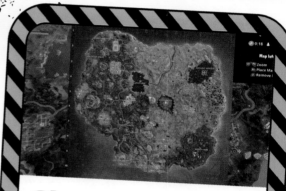

The Map

The map in Fortnite Battle Royale is huge with loads of areas for you to explore over the course of matches. What's really cool about it though is the fact that it continues to evolve and change with successive season Epic Games releases.

Harvesting Tools

There are loads of Harvesting Tools to unlock in Fortnite Battle Royale for real-world money, but at the outset of the game you start off with a simple Pickaxe. Harvesting Tools are absolutely essential for smashing trees, rocks and buildings to gather materials required for building during matches.

Building Materials

There are three types of Building Materials that can be harvested in Fortnite Battle Royale. These are Wood – this is the most common material available, Brick - which isn't as common as Wood, but more durable, and Metal - a material that provides maximum protection during a battle with another player.

Looting

When you land on the main island you have no weapons save for the Harvesting Tool. This can save your life if you're duelling with a weapon-less enemy, but the key to survival in Fortnite Battle Royale is looting locations to get the best weapons and items.

Weapons

There are five different rarity types of weapons in Fortnite Battle Royale. Rarities are colour coded to help you understand the stats of each of the guns scattered around the map. Gray is Common, Green is Uncommon, Blue is Rare, Purple is Epic and Orange is Legendary, which also happens to be the best weapon type there is.

Explosive Weapons

Explosive Weapons are perfect for taking down enemy fortifications in battle. They come in a variety of styles, including RPGs, Grenade Launchers, Guided Missiles, Impulse Grenades, Boogie Bombs, standard Grenades and Remote Explosives. Like other weapon classes they come in a series of Rarity Classes.

Communication

Communication is key in Fortnite Battle Royale. That's why it's essential to wear a headset if you're playing in a squad of two or four players. If you can't communicate chances are you're not going to last very long on the battlefield. Always watch your teammate's backs, and ask them to do the same for you.

Healing

There are lots of ways to heal in Fortnite Battle Royale, including Bandages, Med Kits, Shield Potions, Chug Jugs, Slurp Juice and Cosy Campfires. If your Shield runs out you'll start to take damage to your Health Bar, so always make sure you have a steady supply as the match draws to an end.

Storm Eye

Once a match has begun you're given a certain amount of time to loot for weapons and gear before the Storm Eye warning is sounded. Storm Eyes are lethal, so you don't want to be caught inside one or it will deplete your health, so always keep an eye on the map and countdown timer to avoid dying in one.

V Is For Victory!

At the end of the day in Fortnite Battle Royale the goal is to win a match either on your own or with a group of other players. Winning can be hard when you're starting out in the game, so have patience and use early matches to hone both your combat and building skills. Once you do that, you should be ready to hit the road to victory!

21

THE BATTLE PASS

A guide to the **Battle Pass** and how it works in Fortnite Battle Royale.

WHAT IS THE BATTLE PASS?

Battle Passes are released at the start of every season in Fortnite Battle Royale. The Battle Pass works on two tiers, silver and gold, with silver being free and gold requiring you to purchase the Battle Pass at the outset of each new season.

SILVER TIER

Sticking with the Silver Tier costs nothing and every player is granted access to it at the outset of the season in Fortnite Battle Royale. Rewards in Silver Tier are unlocked every four levels, and include items such as emotes and cosmetic harvesting tools.

GOLD TIER

If you're a regular player of Fortnite Battle Royale then picking up the Battle Pass is definitely worth it. It costs 950 V-Bucks and opens up the Gold Tier bonuses, which includes costumes and Experience Points boosts coupled with rewards for levelling up.

LEVEL UP YOUR BATTLE PASS

To level up your Battle Pass all you need to do is play matches and complete daily challenges to earn Experience Points. Experience Points, or XP, get you Battle Stars. The more Battle Stars you earn the more you get back from your Battle Pass.

EARN EXPERIENCE POINTS

You can earn Experience Points in Fortnite Battle Royale as you play the game by winning Battle Royale matches, taking out other players on the battlefield and simply surviving for a certain amount of time during the wild 100 player matches.

EARN BATTLE STARS

Battle Stars are earned each time you level up throughout a season. Each level grants one Battle Star, but to encourage you to keep playing you get five bonus Battle Stars every five levels and ten Battle Stars every time you reach ten levels.

EXPERIENCE POINTS BOOST

One of the great things about picking up the Battle Pass is the Experience Point Boost, which unlocks after you've reached a certain level in the season, increasing the rate you earn those coveted Battle Stars in Battle Royale mode.

BUY THE BATTLE PASS

Picking up the Battle Pass is really simple: power up the game, look for the Battle Pass tab in the menu, hit Purchase and follow the on-screen instructions to gain access to it and all the awesome rewards tethered to each season's Battle Pass.

V-BUCKS

Take a **deep-dive** into the shiny world of V-Bucks, Fortnite's in-game currency.

Fortnite Battle Royale won't cost you a penny to download, but that doesn't mean there aren't ways to spend real-world cash on in-game goodies as well as other items to spice things up on the battlefield. That said it's important to note that these items simply alter the visual appearance of your character and do not give you a gameplay advantage. Let's take a look at all the things you can do with V-Bucks, as well as how to earn them in the full game, Fortnite: Save The World.

Fortnite Save The World

Arguably the most consistent way to earn V-Bucks in Fortnite is through purchasing Fortnite: Save The World, and playing the game's PvE Horde Mode. Once you have picked up a copy of Save The World you can earn V-Bucks for taking part in the game's different activities, and whatever you accumulate is then transferred over to your Battle Royale character.

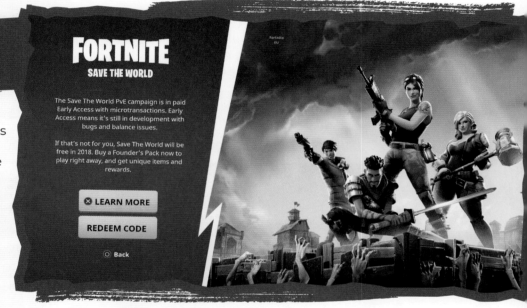

The Real Cost of V-Bucks

Okay, so V-Bucks are a fictional currency in the world of Fortnite, but what are they worth in terms of real world money? Depending on your budget V-Bucks come in multiple packages. At the time of writing 1,000 will cost you £7.99, 2,500 costs £19.99, 6,000 equates to £49.99 and 10,000 will set you back a hefty £79.99.

Daily Log-Ins

One easy way to earn V-Bucks once you've got Save The World is to simply login every day. Even if you don't feel like playing the game, just booting up your console or desktop computer and logging into the game to claim your V-Bucks is worth it, because Daily Login Rewards range anywhere from 50 to 1000 V-Bucks.

Daily Quests

Performing Daily Quests are a great way of earning V-Bucks once you have purchased Save The World. Each day you login you'll get a new Daily Quest to take on. Rewards for performing each one tend to range anywhere from 50 V-Bucks per Quest to 100 V-Bucks. The Quests range from smashing particular items to completing missions and wiping out certain enemies on the battlefield.

Special Offers

From time to time stores such as Game offer up cool incentives to earn V-Bucks, including one such event that took place earlier in the year where all you had to do was use your Game Reward Card while making a purchase online or in-store. Once you did that you were then entered into a draw to win 50 V-Bucks. Nice!

Storm Shield Defence Missions

Storm Shield Defence Missions are excellent V-Buck generators in Save The World. These bombastic missions are located all around the Save The World Map, and there are usually at least five to beat in all of the game areas. You can't do them alone, so get some friends to battle alongside you or team up with other players from the world.

Purchasing V-Bucks

There are lots of ways to purchase V-Bucks, including buying directly from the Microsoft Store, PlayStation Store and the Nintendo eShop, or from the App Store on your mobile device. Other options include purchasing Gift Cards for each of the stores depending on what device you're playing the game on. If you're purchasing from a third party site such as eBay and the price of V-Bucks seems too good to be true, then that probably means it is so be careful.

Watch Out For Scams!

Listen up because this one is important – THERE IS NO SUCH THING AS FREE V-BUCKS IN FORTNITE. Do not under any circumstances give your account details to any website or person claiming to offer up free V-Bucks, because they are trying to scam you. Epic Games have had to address this matter in the past, so it's something that does happen from time to time.

Add To The Collection

Much like the Daily Login bonuses you can also earn V-Bucks for levelling up your Collection Book. Unfortunately trying to earn V-Bucks this way does tend to take a lot of time. If you're prepared to put the work in then you'll wrack up V-Bucks at Level 6, Level 26 and Level 91 with each one nabbing you 500 in total.

Timed Missions

Timed Missions are a rarity in terms of generating V-Bucks and you have to be quick to get to them. They appear on the map of Save The World and tend to have a ticking clock attached to them. Most of the time the rewards involve pure drops of rain or ore missions. You can only compete in three timed missions a day.

Buy A Llama

When you play Fortnite: Save The World the best way of grabbing cool stuff that you can use to kit your characters out in-game is to purchase a Llama, but be warned not all Llamas are packed with the best items, so choose wisely when making a purchase. Llamas appear in the Battle Royale mode, but these only include building materials and not V-Bucks.

Buy The Battle Pass

Battle Passes can be purchased for 950 V-Bucks, and with each one you get a plethora of rewards including special skins and emotes. However, these skins are not available right away, you have to earn them by playing the game and unlocking each one. Buying a Battle Pass does cost real world money, but if you've already earned that amount through playing the game it's worth buying.

GET IN CHARACTER

While pretty much the entire world spends its time playing Fortnite Battle Royale's 100v100 mode, there are still a large, and loyal, number of gamers grinding their way through the Save The World campaign, which was released back in the summer of 2017.

If you're not familiar with this element of Fortnite, it's the part of the game currently in Early Access and will set you back £32.99 for The Standard Founders Pack, or £49.99 for the Deluxe Founders Pack, at the time of writing. Unlike the simplicity of Fortnite Battle Royale mode, Save The World can be quite complicated starting out if you're unfamiliar with the different Hero Classes and their Sub Classes available to you in the game.

The most important thing to remember before delving into the character classes in the game is that each one mirrors differing styles of play. What that means is certain classes are better suited to certain players such as those who prefer stealth over those who might err on the side of a blazing gun approach to things.

SOLDIER

The All-Rounder

At the outset of Save The World everyone starts out as a Soldier. This is a good thing, because they're the most robust and well-rounded class available. Soldiers possess a nice balance of offense, defence and crafting skills on the battlefield.

They can throw simple structures up in a jiffy, and blast enemies to pieces in a flash with a steady stream of bullets from their assault rifles, or by lobbing grenades or laying down mines to take out waves of incoming bad guys to quickly clear the battlefield and give your team a breather before things heat up again.

There are a number of Sub Classes to pick from, with some of the best being Urban Assault, Special Forces, Commando, Raider and Master Grenadier, who are hard to acquire due to the fact they're part of the Mythic Rarity Sub Class.

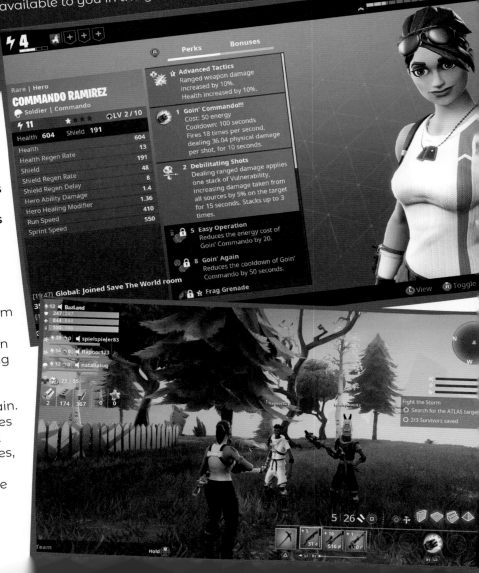

CONSTRUCTOR
The Builder

Perks   Bonuses

L1 R1

mmon | Hero

E KYLE
nstructor | BASE

★★★   ⬆LV 1/10

538   Shield 199

n	538
Regen Rate	13
	199
Regen Rate	50
Regen Delay	8
bility Damage	0.8
ealing Modifier	0.8
eed	410
Speed	550

✦ Creative Engineering
Increases build speed by 10%.
Reduces building cost by 10%.

1 Bull Rush
Cost: 20 energy
Cooldown: 15 seconds
Does 132.3 blunt physical damage. The Constructor charges forward 3 tiles, collecting enemies on a shield, knocking them back at the end of the rush or when colliding with a wall.

🔒 2 BASE
Cost: 100 energy
Cooldown: 4 seconds
The BASE alters the matter of connected building pieces. Affected walls will do energy damage to any enemy that strikes the wall with a melee attack.
Attached structures gain 12% damage resistance.
Extends 3 segments from placement.

Global: Joined Save The World room

🎮 Hold to chat

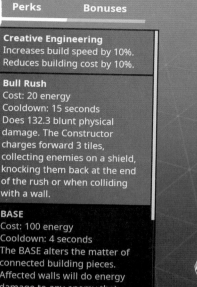

LEVEL UP AVAILABLE!

⬆   6,430 / 150

Ⓐ Level Up

Fortnite Save The World is all about building, which means the Constructor is definitely one of the best choices if you're looking to master the art of building and throw up structures to defend your team from attacks. Constructors are experts at repairing, fortifying and crafting structures to control incoming waves of enemies during missions.

These Hero characters are able to build much faster than the other Heroes, and don't use up as many resources either. They also possess a nifty ability called B.A.S.E that allows them to increase the strength of the fortifications they craft. While not the fastest Hero Class, they can still take a beating in battle and put up a decent fight.

The best Constructor Sub Classes to look out for in the game are Power BASE, Hotfixer, Controller, Machinist and Megabase, who can amplify the B.A.S.E ability enormously by conjuring electrified floors and walls that reflect damage.

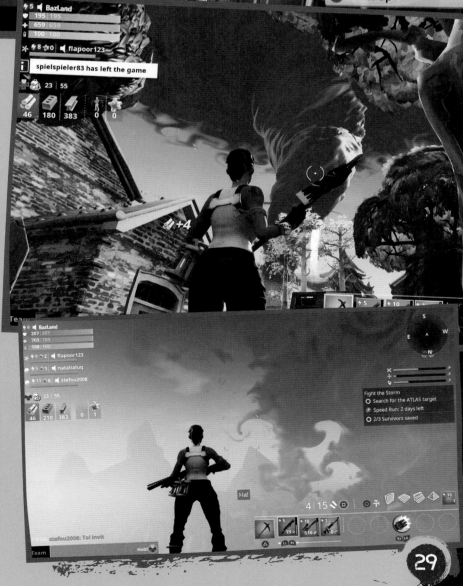

29

NINJA
The Melee Master

BRAWLER LUNA
✦ Ninja | Brawler

⚡ 5 ★★★ ⟰LV 1/10

Health **372**   Shield **191**

Health	372
Health Regen Rate	9
Shield	191
Shield Regen Rate	48
Shield Regen Delay	8
Hero Ability Damage	1.2
Hero Healing Modifier	1.2
Run Speed	452
Sprint Speed	605

Perks   Bonuses

☆ **Shinobi**
Reduces fall damage taken by 10%. Increases run and sprint speed by 10%.

1 Crescent Kick
Cost: 30 energy
Cooldown: 10 seconds
A quick kick that does 70.0 damage, 900.0 impact, and stuns for 3 seconds.

🔒 **2 Mantis Leap**
Cost: 20 energy
Cooldown: 0.5 seconds
Ninja can leap once more while already jumping. Can only be executed once per jump.

🔒 **5 Kickback**
Reduces the energy cost of Crescent Kick by 14.

🔒 **8 Five Winds Cut**
Increases damage of swords, axes, and scythes by 24%.

☆ **Dragon Slash**
Cost: 50 energy

[19:47] **Global: Joined Save The World room** 3513
[19:49] **Aliscott71:** No i have

Global   🎮 Hold to char...

Ⓥ 200   👥 0

⬆ 6,430 / 150

LEVEL UP AVAILABLE!

△ Level Up

ⓛ View   ⓡ Toggle Favorite   ☐ Upgrade   ◯ Back

The Ninja Hero Class is without doubt the fastest of all the Heroes in the game. Yes, they are similar in a sense to the Soldiers in terms of how much damage they can dole out, but rather than relying on big, burly heavy Assault Rifles the Ninjas instead focus on close-quarter combat with awesome swords and other weapons of the same ilk.

However there is a catch – you need to get up close and personal. This means you're open to attack a lot of the time, and the Ninja's don't have the best of defences either. To counteract this Ninjas can jump much higher thanks to the Mantis Leap, so if you pick this Hero be sure to bounce around the battlefield to avoid getting swarmed.

The top Sub Classes are the Swordmaster, Shuriken Master and Dragon, who is the most powerful thanks to a big power boost and the mighty Dragon Slash attack.

OUTLANDER

The Gatherer

If you're a loot-lover kind of gamer, then the Outlander is most definitely for you. These Heroes are all about harvesting materials on the map. One of the great things about them is they can sniff out Loot Chests with the Keen Eye ability.

Outlanders aren't the best warriors if you're keen on mowing down enemies, but they do possess some gadget-based abilities like being able to drop a sentry gun in the shape of a teddy bear that can mow monsters down. These Heroes are really designed for team players, so if you go down this route you'll be spending a lot of time bouncing around the battlefield grabbing supplies for your squad.

There are some great Outlander Heroes to choose from, including Ranger who can wield a pistol like a boss, and bash out critical hit after critical hit. Other good choices are Recon Scout or Pathfinder who are the best of the bunch.

SUPER

SKINS!

Skins for your character in Fortnite Battle Royale are a big deal. They come in all shapes, sizes, and rarities, and seeing other players with the latest and greatest getup makes us green with envy. But it's worth noting that playing the game wearing the same outfit as other players isn't really going to affect your performance in a match, but if you want to get your hands on new skins you're ultimately going to have to hand over your hard earned cash to unlock them.

There are numerous ways to do this – you can purchase the Battle Pass, which unlocks outfits as you progress through matches, or you can simply head to the Item Store and spend some V-Bucks to buy an outfit to wear in your next game. One of the big things to remember is that costumes appear in the store for a limited time only, and only some of them are brought back briefly, so if you see something you like you need to act fast and grab it or it could be gone forever.

Without further ado, here are some of the coolest costumes we've come across during our time battling the masses in the wild world of Fortnite Battle Royale!

1 Highland Warrior

There can only be one! Actually, there can be 99, but who's counting? The Highland Warrior is part of the Laoch set, and perfect for players with a penchant for Braveheart battle cries.

2 Battle Shroud

This mysterious and legendary looking warrior of the battlefield is shrouded in mystery and part of the Overseer set. If you want to look like a scary superhero then this outfit is the one for you.

3 Wingman

The Wingman is readily available on games stores and quite cheap considering you get yourself a sharp looking outfit, 600 V-bucks and a slick Bogey Back Bling. We've seen this on the battlefield a lot, but that doesn't make it any less cool.

4 Oblivion

This Oblivion getup is super threatening on the battlefield with its sleek design that is part superhero, part cyborg. It also comes with a very stylish back bling. If you feel like wreaking vengeance on enemies, this is the outfit for you.

5 Burnout

Vroom, vroom! The Burnout costume reminds us of that classic Sega Megadrive game, Road Rash, and really makes us wish Epic Games would introduce motorbikes into the game in a future update. Ride or die Battle Royale fans!

6 Ventura

Part of the Venture set, Ventura looks like a steampunk superhero especially with those big and wild blue goggles on that slick mask of hers. Apparently, if you wear this then you are destined for greatness!

7 Dynamic Dribbler

This sporty skin is perfect for football fans and was released to celebrate the 2018 World Cup during the summer, so if you didn't manage to snag it the chances are it's not going to be returning anytime soon.

8 Liteshow

Do you like to party? Then Liteshow is the funkiest character skin of them all. Part of the Neon Glow set - and cheap compared to some of the other costumes we've seen on the store - this one's solely for the disco kings.

9 The Reaper

The Reaper is arguably one of your favourite character skins since Fortnite Battle Royale kicked off. Part of the hired gun set, this bad boy bares more than a striking resemblance to movie character, John Wick, played by Keanu Reeves.

10 Magnus

Conquer the storm with Magnus the big, bad bearded Viking. Clad in mighty Viking helmet and a Nordic suit of armour as well as sporting heavily tattooed arms, he was part of the Norse Set and also had a mighty axe for kicking butt.

11 Leviathan

We love this Legendary Leviathan skin that came as part of the Space Explorers set. It features a grinning Piranha inside a fishbowl attached to a spacesuit, and sports a slick animation that sees bubbles pop out of the mouth of the little fanged fiend.

12 Shadow Ops

If you want to remain stealthy throughout your time on the battlefield, then this slick Shadow Ops garb is the one for you. Part of the Stealth Syndicate Set alongside the Midnight Ops skin, this one is heavily inspired by covert super spies. Snag it and they'll never see you coming!

13 Flytrap

Flytrap is terrifying to look at. Part of the Flytrap Set this frightening outfit transforms your character into a super-villain with spikes for hair and razor sharp talons in a super suit that's decorated with alien-like plant roots.

14 Masked Fury

Part of the Lucha Gear set, the Masked Fury takes its design cues from the world of Lucha Libre wrestling, which is really popular in Mexico. The female skin is called Dynamo, and the set also includes Lucha Libre inspired Gliders and Pickaxes.

15 Black Knight

Released all the way back during Season Two of Fortnite Battle Royale, The Black Knight is one scary looking character that's for sure. Sporting an outfit worn by the odious scourge of Wailing Woods, this costume is one of the most sought after items amongst fans of the game.

16 Raven

Alongside the Black Knight the Raven is arguably one of the most intimidating costumes to pick up in Fortnite Battle Royale thanks to its jet-black leather and dark hood that hides everything bar those purple glowing eyes. Part of the Nevermore set, this Legendary outfit is a must-own!

17 Skull Trooper

Released as part of the fearsome Fortnitemares update, the Skull Trooper takes a simple military suit and spooks it up with some creepy paintwork to resemble a skeleton. Break this one out to scare the competition off during play!

18 Dark Vanguard

Part of the Space Explorers set, the Dark Vanguard is a female Legendary outfit sporting an orange vest pattern and pitch-black astronaut helmet that's sure to send enemies running in fear! Anyone who bought this snagged a bonus Back Bling called the Dark Void.

19 Special Forces

This Rare outfit may be kind of simple, but that doesn't mean we still don't love its simplistic soldier-themed design. Rounding off the design is a sweet military black beret, black scarf, army boots and gloves. Like we said, simple but stylish!

20 Sgt. Green Clover

Do ya feel lucky? Well, do ya, punk? Of course you do, because you're wearing the Green Clover set, which was released as an event-only outfit and borrowed its design from the little people found guarding big pots of gold – Leprechauns!

BUILD LIKE A BOSS

Fortnite's Battle Royale mode differentiates itself from the rest of the Battle Royale games on the market with its excellent building system, which takes the game in a whole new direction, especially when the match is coming to an end. Here's to mastering the art of building and taking your fight to a whole new level!

Scavenge On The Go

Staying in the one area to gather materials is a foolish tactic, so always be moving from area to area smashing objects and snagging supplies as you travel from location to location. Almost everything on the map is destructible, so there is no shortage of trees, rocks or abandoned vehicles to scavenge materials from.

Wonderful Wood

Wood, glorious wood! This material is the most common type of supplies you can find in the game. It's ideal for building bridges, stairs to get to hard to reach places, as well as secret locations containing stacks of Legendary and Rare loot. It's also useful for crafting emergency cover if you find yourself in a sticky situation. You can harvest wood from houses, bushes and trees scattered throughout the map.

Brilliant Brick

Brick is the second strongest type of building material in the game. It doesn't quite have the same staying power as metal when it comes to being attacked with explosives, so be aware of that if someone is coming at you with heavy artillery. Brick can be harvested from a variety of sources, including walls, chimneys and stones found out in the open.

Heavy Metal

Metal is by far the strongest type of building material in Fortnite Battle Royale. It can withstand a single blast from an RPG, which makes it ideal for crafting fortifications during the final moments of the game where you're frantically trying to protect yourself and get the jump on the last of your opponents. Grab it from vehicles.

Cover Ramps

Matches are a nerve-wracking experience from start to finish, and there's nothing more terrifying than having to dash across wide-open terrain, especially if you're being chased or you think another player is watching from afar. To ease the tension a little lay down Cover Ramps in all directions to confuse any would-be threats. It'll save your life and drive a potential assassin absolutely crazy!

Who Needs Stairs?

The Map in Fortnite Battle Royale is filled with all sorts of terrain for you to trek across over the course of a match, and at times you'll need to quickly scale a Cliffside by building stairs to the top. Stairs and ramps are also super useful for reaching rooftops on structures that aren't easily accessible to search for loot.

Basic Cover

Let's say you're dashing across an open section of the map, and all of a sudden someone starts shooting at you from behind. It's not a good position to be in, but there is a way out of said situation – simply build a basic wall to use as cover. You'd be surprised how many times doing something like this can save your skin!

Recon Forts

Recon Forts are simple yet extremely effective and essential buildings in Fortnite Battle Royale. They're ideal for when you're approaching a new area and need to get a look around before entering. Simply throw down four walls around you, then drop a ramp under your feet. If you want to go higher just repeat the process.

Sniper Towers

Sniper Towers are perfect for gaining some serious altitude in Fortnite Battle Royale, provided you have a good sniper rifle of course! They don't take much time to build, and are ideal for when you spot an enemy dashing across the map towards a loot spot and want to take them out from a distance.

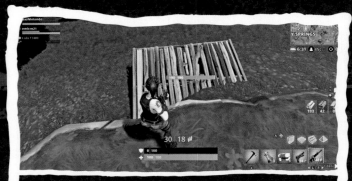

Break Your Fall

If you're running from the Storm Circle, or happen to be the last one standing in your squad and have to slide off the edge of a cliff you can avoid croaking it by quickly dropping floor structures underneath you to avoid taking serious damage. Word of warning: you need to be quick off the mark to nail this building trick!

Tunnel Ramps

Tunnel Ramps are extremely hard to master, but they can save your life when bullets are zinging over your head in every direction. To build one, drop a wall so that you have something to anchor the Tunnel Ramp to. From there throw down some ramps above and below at the same time, which is tricky!

Edit, Edit, Edit!

If you've built a structure that's a bit of a mess, especially during a frantic battle, you can always edit your way out of a sticky situation. For example, if someone has found their way inside your structure make a hole in the floor to drop down and take them out in Battle Royale style.

Transparent Walls

If you've built yourself a fort or tower to save your skin in the midst of a massive fire-fight and are surrounded on all sides by encroaching enemies the best way to get a view of what's happening on the outside is to use the Edit Tool to remove sections of the wall, because if you don't finalize the edit it will return to normal.

A Quiet Place

If you're low on health it's not a smart idea to whip out Med Kit or Bandages and start healing out in the open. The smartest way to replenish low energy is to build four walls around you for cover, and then use an item, but don't forget to listen out for approaching footsteps!

Sky High

As the match comes to an end and that dastardly storm starts to close in on you and the other players it means space on the battlefield is limited. To get around this simply build upward piling on the ramps and walls so that you can reach a great vantage point and spot incoming foes.

WEAPONS OF MASS DESTRUCTION

If you really want to kick butt in Fortnite Battle Royale you have to spend some time getting to grips with each of the weapons on offer in the game, of which there are quite a few. In most situations whatever weapon you have to hand can sometimes save the day, but some of the firepower on offer in the game is decidedly better than others, so we're here to help you figure out which ones you should skip and which ones you should definitely pick up on the battlefield.

Besides walking you through the most essential weaponry worth grabbing while looting, we've also put together some pro tips for you to take into consideration that will hopefully help you understand what weapons you should use and when!

THE GUNS GUIDE
Eight quick tips for weapons looting when you land!

Weapon Rarities

The most important thing to understand about weapons in Fortnite Battle Royale is their rarity type, and which colours are associated with each one. Starting with the weakest and ending with the most powerful, the rarities are: Grey is Common, Green is Uncommon, Blue is Rare, Purple is Epic and Orange Legendary. Memorize those colours!

Grab An Assault Rifle

The first thing you need to do when you hit the ground after jumping from that Battle Bus is to find yourself an Assault Rifle. It doesn't matter which type you grab, just be sure to find one in a building, structure or Loot Chest as soon as possible. Assault Rifles are excellent ranged and close ranged combat weapons.

Find A Shotgun

Next up find a shotgun to sit alongside your Assault Rifle. With the Rifle to hand you'll have a good rate of fire at range, but with the Shotgun you've got a huge advantage when things get up close and personal. You can usually floor an opponent with a blast or two of the Shotgun when things get a little tight.

Switch 'em Up

You can't use a Shotgun at long distance range, or whip out your Sniper Rifle up close; it's lunacy. Switch between weapons in your backpack depending on the situation unfolding in front of you. Find a gun you like to use at a distance. Then find one you're comfortable with in close quarters and fall back on that when the situation calls for it.

Pack Smart

When things are quiet and you've nabbed a whole host of weapons take a moment to open up your backpack and rearrange your arsenal so that it's easy to get to the weapon needed for the situation. For example, have your Assault Rifle and Shotgun next to each other at the front so it'll just take a quick button tap to tool up and blast someone.

It's Definitely You!

At the end of every match there are always players throwing up huge structures to gain the high ground so that they can pick off any stragglers running around the battlefield. To get around this if you happen to be down low be sure to have a Mini Gun in your arsenal, because these things are absolute monsters, they will rip a structure to shreds in seconds.

Silent But Deadly

Silenced weapons are an excellent option if you want to get the jump on someone who is either looting in a building, gathering materials or caught up in a shootout of their own. Shots from a silenced weapon are harder to place if someone if taking fire from another direction, and in most cases you can get the kill before they know it's you!

B Is For Burst

Once you get a handle on aiming try switching from the standard Assault Rifle to a Burst Rifle. These things can be a tad tricky to get used to at the start, but they're excellent for taking down enemies if you can place those shots. One of these at a medium to long-range distance can really shred an enemy's health to pieces.

TOP 10 WEAPONS

Here's our pick of some of the coolest weapons in Fortnite Battle Royale.

1. SUPRESSED PISTOL

The Suppressed Pistol isn't really adequate for long-range shootouts, but it's more than suited to those moments when you're skulking around a building and want to sneak up on someone from behind for a quick and deadly takedown.

2. ASSAULT RIFLE

Assault Rifles are essentials for ranged combat. If you find an Epic or Legendary Rarity one on the battlefield, you're in for a treat, because these things are some of the best guns in the game.

3. HEAVY SHOTGUN

The Heavy Shotguns are excellent for when you want to get up close and personal in a battle. Don't try and use these ones in a ranged firefight; you may land a couple of pellets, but won't last long.

4. DUAL PISTOLS

Dual Pistols aren't the best weapons in the game for ranged combat, but in the hands of someone with a good shot it's possible to win a match. It's not easy to do, but we've seen it being done out there!

5. SCOPED ASSAULT RIFLE

We're back to the Assault Rifles, which are one of the most essential weapons on the battlefield. Now, add a scope to that and you've got yourself a serious advantage in a match when you spot someone in the distance.

6. BOOGIE BOMB

Boogie Bombs aren't like normal hand grenades that simply blow up when they land next to a player; instead they explode in a flurry of dazzling lights forcing players to dance. If caught in it they can't fire, build or use items.

7. SEMI-AUTO SNIPER RIFLE

Semi-Auto Sniper Rifles aren't as powerful as a Bolt-Action Sniper Rifle or Hunting Rifle, but they do hold more bullets and are excellent for rapid-fire shots at enemies wandering around the map in the distance, while you're in a Sniper Tower.

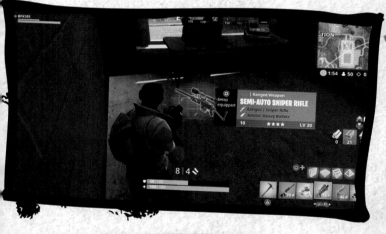

8. MINIGUN

The Minigun is perfect for absolutely shredding other player's structures if they've got a height advantage on you. The only issue with them is that it takes a second or so for the gun to start spitting bullets, so remember that when using one.

9. GRENADE LAUNCHER

The Grenade Launcher is super powerful, but it does come with some caveats – it's tough to master, because you've got to adjust trajectory according to your target. If you can get to grips with that aspect then it's perfect for blowing stuff up!

10. ROCKET LAUNCHER

KABOOM! When all else fails just find yourself one of these bad boys on the battlefield and start taking enemies out left, right and centre. RPGs have excellent range, and best of all your teammates can ride the rocket!

43

FORTNITE FACTS

Fortnite Battle Royale is a gaming **phenomenon**. Here are ten awesome nuggets of information for you to impress your friends with next time you're playing!

1) MOBILE MADNESS

Fortnite Battle Royale was released in March of 2018 on iOS devices including the iPhone and iPad, and in just 96 hours the game earned Epic Games a whopping one million pounds from in-App purchases. How crazy is that?

4) THE REVEAL

Save The World was first revealed to the world all the way back in 2011 at the Spike Video Game Awards, before going extremely quiet until 2014 when it was re-revealed by Epic Games and billed as a free-to-play game.

2) THANOS ATTACKS!

In May of 2018 Fortnite Battle Royale crossed over with Avengers: Infinity War film to bring super villain Thanos into the fold. Once players found the Infinity Gauntlet they were then able to control Thanos and reign down chaos on other players.

5) MEGABUCKS

Streaming is huge, so huge in fact that Twitch streamer Tyler 'Ninja' Blevins said he manages to earn a gargantuan $500,000 per month from playing Battle Royale through fan donations. With 5 million followers on the channel that's a lot of cash!

3) CELEBRITY FANS

Fortnite Battle Royale has a host of celebrity followers, including rappers Drake and Travis Scott, as well as musician and actor Joe Jonas. Even Stranger Things and IT star Finn Wolfhard gets in on the action in between his busy shooting schedule.

6) MOST KILLS!

Back in July 2018 Fortnite player Elemental Ray broke the record for most solo kills in a Battle Royale match when he smashed a platform filled with 48 players who built it in order to watch the special rocket launch event during Season Four.

7) RIVALRIES

Fortnite Battle Royale isn't the only massively multiplayer online game on the market. In fact the game's biggest rival is PlayerUnknown's Battleground, a grittier, darker and arguably more violent take on the Battle Royale formula.

8) UNREAL ENGINE

The game was developed by Epic Games using their Unreal 4 game engine, the same engine used to power the likes of Gears of War 4, Injustice 2, Street Fighter V and the awesome prison break co-op thriller, A Way Out.

10) HAIL TO THE KING!

The Battle Royale mode launched in September 2017 and the numbers were huge. After one day it had amassed one million players, and within just two weeks the player count rose to a whopping 10 million unique users. Holy moly!

9) KERCHING!

When the game was first released in July 2017 it was pretty much an instant hit for Epic Games selling over 500,000 digital copies in a single month. The following month those numbers doubled. And that was all without Battle Royale mode!

EVERYTHING IS EPIC!

Epic Games is arguably one of the most **powerful studios** in the world right now thanks to the success of Fortnite. Let's take a step back in time to chart the rise of one of the world's greatest developers.

Epic Games was born all the way back in 1991 in Potomac, Maryland in the home of Tim Sweeney's parents under the alias of Potomac Computer Systems. The company, and Sweeney's, first release was a simplistic little action-adventure puzzle game titled ZZT. Even back in 1991 it looked a little dated in terms of visuals, but the game still managed to secure a loyal following in the modding community, who could create new levels and game modes with the editor tools included in the game.

Thanks to ZZT's success Sweeney was able to maintain a steady stream of income and come up with his next plan – taking the company to the next level. In early 1992 Potomac Computer Systems changed its name to Epic MegaGames, which Sweeney came up with in order to make his pint-sized company sound like it was a much larger company that could compete with games industry heavy hitters at the time, including id Software, the creators of the monstrous first-person shooter hit Doom.

Time to get unreal

With Epic MegaGames established Sweeney began searching for a

Jill of the Jungle

business partner with the smarts to help elevate the company to the next level. That man was Mark Rein, who joined Sweeney after leaving his role at id Software to take over sales, marketing and publishing deals at Sweeney's burgeoning company.

Jazz Jackrabbit

Deus Ex

Deus Ex

Games such as **Brix**, **Jill of the Jungle** and **One Must Fall: 2097** followed once Rein had joined the company, but it was **Jazz Jackrabbit**, which hit PC in 1994, that heralded a new era for the company, which included the arrival of one of the game world's biggest and coolest personalities, Cliff Bleszinski.

Jazz Jackrabbit was a platform title that mixed elements of Sonic The Hedgehog with a gun-toting rabbit that had to battle his way across multiple worlds to save Princess Eva Earlong. Bleszinski would remain with the company for the next 20 years, playing an integral role in the creation of Epic Mega Games' world-dominating titles, the first of which was fast-paced first-person shooter, **Unreal**, which was designed in direct response to the mammoth success of id Software's Doom II.

Unreal was released on PC in 1998 and quickly became a smash-hit, so much so id Software responded by rush-releasing Quake III, which followed just one year after Quake II arrived in gamers' hands. Unreal was fast, furious and had gamers hooked from the get-go thanks to its flashy visuals and excellent multiplayer mode.

Super powered engine

Besides being a superb game Unreal also had something special under the hood – the Unreal Engine, which powered the game

Unreal

and was considered a huge technical achievement in the gaming community. The company decided to capitalise on this by packaging up the software and licensing it out to other developers, who would in turn use it to build games such as **Deus Ex**, Clive Barker's **Undying** and **Rune**.

The game engine still remains one of the most popular tools in game development and has been responsible for some of the greatest titles ever released on the likes of Xbox and PlayStation, including the **Batman Arkham** series, **Bioshock** and **Splinter Cell**. Riding high on the success of Unreal and Unreal Engine Epic MegaGames changed its named to Epic Games and relocated to Cary, North Carolina where it has remained to this day.

Sequels to Unreal followed soon after, including the critically acclaimed **Unreal Tournament** and **Unreal Championship** on the original Xbox, which would serve as a precursor to the arrival of Epic Games on the world's stage as one of the most important Xbox game developers ever thanks to a little game called Gears of War.

Unreal

Arkham City

Unreal 3

Bulletstorm

Cranking it up a gear

In 2006 the team released **Gears of War**, which was published by Microsoft Studios for the Xbox 360. Gears of War became a gargantuan success for both the studio and Microsoft, turning both the developer and its main character, Marcus Fenix, into game world rock stars. It was the fastest selling game of that year, nabbed countless Game of the Year awards and wound up selling millions of copies right up until the arrival of the sequel, **Gears of War 2**, in 2008.

The success of the Gears of War series and Unreal Engine allowed the company to make a number of acquisitions, including purchasing the Polish developer, People Can Fly, who would go on to develop the first-person shooter, **Bulletstorm**, and Chair Entertainment, and create the Xbox Live Arcade hit, **Shadow Complex** as well as the **Infinity Blade** series on iOS.

In 2011 **Gears of War 3** hit shelves, which ultimately became the last game in the series to be developed by Epic Games, who then shifted focus onto developing their greatest achievement to date, which was revealed to the world at the 2011 Spike Video Game

Gears of War 2

Awards... The colossal multiplayer extravaganza Fortnite!

Fortnite and the future

While the game was certainly a success Epic took notice of the huge popularity of PlayerUnknown's Battlegrounds and began working on its own Battle Royale mode for Fortnite. This free expansion of the game was released in September of 2017 amassing huge numbers of players in a very short time and, well, the rest is gaming history. What does the future hold for Epic Games? Fortnite. Lots of Fortnite, which is more than alright with us and the rest of the fans of the world's most popular and awesome Battle Royale video game.

Splinter Cell

MAKE YOUR WAY DOWN

Splinter Cell

70 m

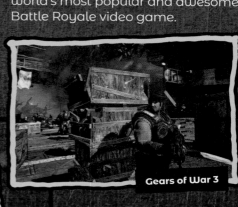

Gears of War 3

THE TEN BEST EPIC GAMES

Check out these essential Epic titles released over the years!

4) Bulletstorm (2011)

Bulletstorm is a whacky shooter that places you in the boots of Grayson Hunt, a space pirate on the run from a crazed general who betrayed him years ago.

8) Infinity Blade II (2011)

Infinity Blade II raised the bar once more in terms of what people thought could be done visually and mechanically on the iPhone with breathtaking combat and narrative.

1) Unreal (1998)

Take on the role of Prisoner 849 and explore spooky prison spacecrafts and uncharted planets while battling monstrous alien beings called the Nali.

5) Gears of War 2 (2008)

The fight against the dreaded Locust Horde continues as Marcus Fenix and his team have to battle the clock to stop their monstrous foes from sinking a city.

9) Unreal Tournament III (2007)

Delve deep into multiplayer madness with a wide variety of bombastic modes, including Duel, Warfare, Greed and Betrayal in one of the best entries in the series.

2) Gears of War (2006)

Grab your Lancer, rev your chainsaw and dive into one of the most ferocious thrilling, and addictive third-person shooters ever to hit Microsoft's Xbox 360.

6) Gears of War 3 (2011)

Strap your boots on for the spectacular final chapter of Marcus Fenix's epic journey as he and his team face a new and even deadlier enemy – the Lambent!

10) Robo Recall

Epic Game' first foray in the world of virtual reality is packed with action as you take on the role of Agent 34 and battle waves of crazed robots.

3) Infinity Blade (2010)

Infinity Blade mixes brawling with exploration and it was the first game to showcase the true potential of Unreal Engine running on a mobile device.

7) Shadow Complex (2009)

Take on the role of Jason Fleming in a mysterious underground complex in a story filled with countless twists and turns, as well as tonnes of action!

EPIC GAMES

25 SURVIVAL TIPS

Millions of gamers are playing Fortnite Battle Royale, all with differing levels of skills. This 100-player mode can be daunting when it comes to learning the ropes, which is why we've compiled these essential survival tips to help you!

1 Avoid Popular Locations

Play it smart, stay away from some of the more popular areas of the map where other players swarm to, such as Tilted Towers. Landing in quieter areas gives you time to loot without the fear of being blasted in the first two minutes of a match.

2 Land Faster

As soon as you skydive from the Battle Bus push down and forward to speed up your descent dramatically. Once you get close enough to the ground the glider will open, then you want to come in diagonally to the landing zone you've chosen.

3 Aim For The Rooftops

Landing on rooftops is an excellent way to get the good loot, because a lot of the time Chests will spawn in the attics of buildings, so all you have to do is smash your way through. It's safer to work your way down to the ground floor too.

4 Be Gear Smart

It's always tempting to grab every piece of loot at the outset of a match, but don't go filling your gear slots up with the same gun. Swap items in and out as you come across the good stuff throughout the matches, especially higher stat guns.

5 Fight Or Flight

Be smart when it comes to gun battles. If you're wielding a puny pistol or a mediocre machine gun and you come across another player with an RPG and an overpowered shotgun you might want to either a) hide or b) run if they spot you!

6 Listen, And Listen Carefully!

Do you own a pair of gaming headphones? If the answer is no, then you really need to invest in some, because listening out for footsteps is essential to survival in the world of Fortnite Battle Royale, so that you're not blasted in the back.

7 Shut The Front Door!

See that house or building you're about to go inside and raid for loot? Shut the door behind you. If another player sees it open they might try creeping up on you. If they see it closed they might think it's empty, which means you'll hear it open.

8 Downed Enemies

In Squad Mode and Duo Mode players do not die once you gun them down. They can be revived by their teammates, so don't be tempted to run in to finish them off until you're absolutely certain their friends aren't coming to save them.

9 Downed Teammates

If you're playing with a teammate and an opposing squad member downs them, don't run straight towards your friend to revive them. Reviving leaves you massively exposed to attacks, and chances are it's most likely a trap to lure you out into the open. Take a moment, look around for signs of the enemy and only then help them out!

10 Recon

Be smart - don't run straight into a building, house or area of the map you haven't taken the time to check out. Look for signs of structures other players have built, scan for open doors and build a Recon Fort to protect yourself from attacks.

11 Heal Up, Shield Up!

If health is running low don't wait until you get to the next area to heal, do it immediately. If you have a shield potion don't let it sit in your inventory if you have no shield – use it now. It's no good to you if someone's taken you out!

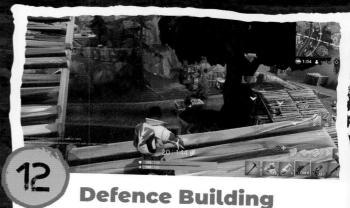

12 Defence Building

Learning to build and build quickly is an essential part of Battle Royale, because in the heat of combat you're going to need to able to protect yourself by throwing up cover and defensive buildings. Remember, wood is easy to destroy!

13 Height Is Might

As the player count dwindles and the Storm Eye shrinks you'll see structures flying up left, right and centre. You should be doing the very same thing to gain a height advantage. If someone is on the ground you'll be able to take them out.

14 Storm Savvy

If you get caught in a Storm your health depletes. Shields won't protect you here, so always keep an eye out for where the circle is and how long you have to get to the next safe zone before it hits. Stick to the edge of safe zones to buy time too.

15 Blow Stuff Up!

If you find yourself inside one of the final safe zones and there are players camped out in sniper towers or huge structures, do the smart thing and just blow them up to take them out. That's why it's important to search for explosive weapons!

53

16 Stay Low

A great way to lower the sound of your footsteps when sneaking around buildings is to crouch down. It's also a great way to get the jump on players too busy to hear you creeping up on them. Crouching also helps when there are snipers!

17 Player Loot

Let's say you've taken another player out and they drop a bunch of cool loot, don't go running to grab it. Look around and watch for their teammates to make sure you aren't surprised by the rest of the squad and lose all of that sweet stuff!

18 Grab A Hop Rock

Keep an eye out for Hop Rocks as you explore the map. They're the blue glowing rocks that let players jump around the map with awesome low-gravity physics. Hop Rocks are also great for pulling off sweet mid-air trick shots on unsuspecting enemies.

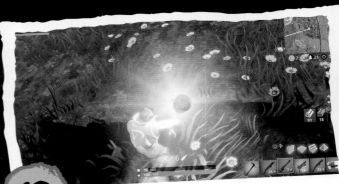

19 Have A Snack

If you're running low on health with no healing gear have a look for fallen apples. These tasty little snacks will replenish a smidgen of health, which might wind up saving your life, whereas the Blue Mushrooms will boost your shield just a little.

20 Search Chests

Hear that strange hum coming from somewhere? That means there's a Loot Chest hidden nearby, usually behind a wall or in an attic. Seek them out, because these things are always loaded with some of the best gear there is to find in the game.

21 Learn To Build Fast

It can be really daunting the first time you play Fortnite Battle Royale. There's so much to learn, so spend time at the start of your journey landing in quiet areas to practice your building skills so that you can throw up structures quickly.

22 Use Cover

If you find yourself in the midst of a fire-fight use cover if it's available. If it's not then just build some. Turning on your heel and running isn't a good idea, because you're likely to take a round of bullets in the back, ending your match.

23 Colour Codes

All of the weapons in Fortnite Battle Royale are colour-coded for stat quality so that you know which ones are the best to grab in the middle of a looting blitz. The scale goes from grey to orange, with grey weapons possessing the worst stats.

24 Pro Controller Settings

Struggling with the controls in Fortnite Battle Royale? Don't fret. They can be a tad tricky, but there is a way to improve this by switching to Pro Controller Settings. To change them, open the Main Menu, choose Settings and then select Controller Settings.

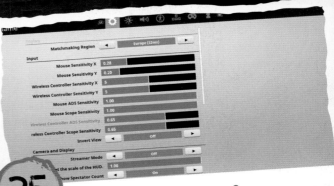

25 Tests Your Settings

Long-time PC players tweak Sensitivity Settings for a better gaming experience and faster reaction times, but if you're playing on console you might never consider this. Try experimenting with these in the Settings Menu to find out what works best for you on the battlefield.

FAST AND THE FURIOUS

Ten tips and things to do in Fortnite Battle Royale's **All Terrain Kart!**

1 Driving

Once you find an All Terrain Kart press the Drive Button to take the wheel. You can also switch seats with your teammates if you don't feel like driving, as well as power slide, which grants you a minor speed boost. That one's useful in a chase!

2 Riding Shotgun

If you manage to call shotgun while your teammate takes the wheel have your gun at the ready and spin that camera around as much as possible so that you are constantly checking the surroundings. This is super-important in Duo mode!

3 The Fab Foursome

The best thing about the All Terrain Kart is that you can fit your entire squad into it, which means you and your teammates can blast across huge chunks of the map super-fast. It's also great for outrunning the Storm Eye if it's on your tail.

4 Backseat Passenger

Don't want to drive? Then get in back and have your gun at the ready so that you can defend the driver from incoming attacks should other squads spot you cruising in the ATK. Don't forget to shield-up, because you'll be exposed!

5 The Scenic Route

If you find yourself behind the wheel of an ATK and you're all alone in a quiet section of the map while other players go toe-to-toe with each other take your time and go for a relaxing drive through the Fortnite countryside to take it all in.

6 Jump

If you really want to have some fun why not build a ramp and hit the gas to see how far you can soar through the air in an ATK. If you've got rear passengers they can help you jump higher by leaning back just before you hit the jump.

7 Found One

ATKs tend to spawn all over the map, but if you're adamant on getting one right off the bat head to Lazy Links and the Racetrack where they are likely to spawn more regularly in areas such as the car showroom or the Racetrack car park.

8 Let's Race!

If you're playing Duos or Squads grab an ATK and challenge your teammates to a race across the map, or skydive to the Racetrack and put pedal to the metal to see who can cross the finish line first, but watch out for other players!

10 Rollin', Rollin', Rollin'

One of the coolest things about the ATK is that you don't appear to take damage if you're barrelling down a hill and spin out of control, or if you manage to flip the Kart attempting a jump. Go ahead and try it!

9 Ramming Speed!

Feeling dangerous? Jump into an All Terrain Kart, put your foot down and try to ram as many players as you can, but the thing to remember is that you can't shoot, which means you are extremely vulnerable, especially to heavy firepower.

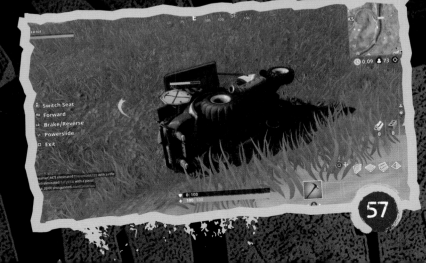

SHOPPING CART SHENANIGANS

Fortnite's **zany** vehicle is unlike any other in the Battle Royale genre!

While Fortnite Battle Royale has featured Limited Time modes of transport, including Jetpacks – which we really want to see make a return – the whacky Shopping Cart looks like it's here to stay, despite some teething problems.

Epic Games certainly had its fair share of headaches whilst implementing the new travelling item into the game. The Carts were originally introduced in May 2018 before being pulled two weeks later due to a bug that allowed players to travel underneath the map. On June 14th 2018 they made a welcome return before being kicked to the kerb two days later.

They didn't return again until June 20th 2018, but just two hours after being reintroduced Epic was forced to pull the plug once more. Sheesh. While this may seem quite funny, the main concern was that players were building pyramids over the Carts and then travelling under the map, which in turn allowed them to see and kill other players above them, which is extremely unfair... and cheating!

Players love the Shopping Carts, and we've seen some crazy stunts being pulled off in them during our time playing the game so here's hoping that Epic doesn't have to remove them yet again, because the cheaters are spoiling it for the fans!

SHOPPING CART TIPS

Everything you need to know about the wheels of steel!

Exposed

The biggest issue with the Shopping Cart is that you're completely exposed while pushing one around, so be sure to rotate the camera and watch your back for enemies trying to get the drop on you.

Controls

When you find a Shopping Cart press the Drive Button to grab hold. To move tap the Push Button, or hold it down to coast along. Tapping the Switch Seat Button lets you leap into the basket.

Find A Friend

Shopping Carts are fun to use on your own, but playing with friends is an absolute blast. Get them to jump inside while you push them off a steep cliff!

Shooting

You can't shoot while pushing the Shopping Cart, but you can leap inside the basket while speeding down a hill or ramp and take shots at enemies attacking you!

Stairs & Hills

You can use the Shopping Cart to travel up hills with a simple tap of the Push Button, but if you've got someone inside it then have them build a ramp or stairs!

FORTNITE

Master the pint-sized version of Epic's, um, epic game on mobile with these ten essential battle tactics.

COMBAT CONTROLS

Drag anywhere to aim

Tap to fire weapon

Double tap + hold to keep firing

Drag to move

Double tap to autorun

Enter Build Mode

Tap to select   Tap to reload

1 COMBAT CONTROLS

Mastering Fortnite on mobile means even the most seasoned of players will have to relearn the games controls considering everything on this iteration is built on a touchscreen control scheme. It takes practice, but be sure to spend some time checking out the tutorial screens that break the controls down in detail.

2 BUILDING CONTROLS

BUILDING CONTROLS

Tap to rotate piece

Tap to edit piece

Tap to place object

Tap to change material   Enter Combat Mode

Building is the bedrock of Fortnite, so don't be tempted to avoid this gameplay aspect while playing the mobile version. That said, it does require you to switch from Combat Mode to Build Mode, so spend some time getting used to flipping between the two. Mastering Building on mobile can save your life in combat.

4 TOUCH SENSITIVITY

Fortnite mobile controls are extremely different from the console and desktop versions of the game. You're going to be swiping the screen a lot to look around, so when you first start playing be sure to keep an eye on how fast your camera movements are. If it's too fast or slow head to the Settings Menu and adjust to fit.

100 18

3 HEADPHONES

Sound is your best friend in Fortnite, so don't be tempted to play the game without a pair of headphones. They're essential for spatial awareness during matches, but if you forgot to pack them for your journey then watch for the visual cues Epic included in this version for situations such as this.

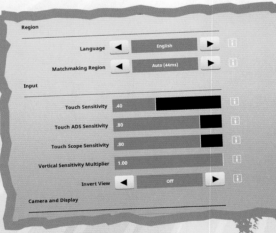

Region

| Language | ◄ | English | ► | ⓘ |
| Matchmaking Region | ◄ | Auto (44ms) | ► | ⓘ |

Input

Touch Sensitivity	.40		ⓘ
Touch ADS Sensitivity	.80		ⓘ
Touch Scope Sensitivity	.80		ⓘ
Vertical Sensitivity Multiplier	1.00		ⓘ
Invert View	◄	Off	►	ⓘ

Camera and Display

5 AUTO RUN

In Fortnite you spend a lot of time running across open areas where attacks can come from any angle. With touch controls you're automatically hindered, because your thumbs are blocking the screen, so double-tap the control stick on the left side of the screen to enable Auto-Run and use a finger to check the area.

6 ADS

The ADS or Aim Down Sights button is located to the left of the Crouch button on your device. Using it will automatically slow your movement, but on mobile versions it's an essential battle tactic, because firing from the hip can cause a serious amount of ammo wastage. For even more accuracy simply crouch down.

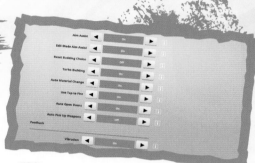

7 RESOURCE MANAGEMENT

In the mobile version characters automatically pick up loot, which means your inventory can fill up quickly. To avoid this problem go to the Settings Menu and hit the Auto Pick Up Weapons option located under the Gear Icon. It'll save you so much time during battle trying to dump low quality items for the good stuff.

8 AVOID CROSS-PLATFORM

With Fortnite on mobile you can cross-play with Xbox, PlayStation 4, PC, Mac and Nintendo Switch, but while it's a pretty slick feature we'd suggest avoiding it for at least the first few matches until you feel confident enough to take on the challenge of competing against players with a superior controller set-up to hand.

10 CLOSE COMBAT

There's a huge difference between playing Fortnite on a massive telly versus a mobile screen, so don't be tempted to take pot shots at players far off in the distance, because all you'll do is alert them. For maximum impact get up close and personal. That way you're more likely to take your opponent down quicker.

9 DON'T SHOOT!

Playing Fortnite on a mobile device or a tablet can be a tad tricky at the outset given the touch-screen controls, so to avoid accidentally blasting off a round quickly switch to your pickaxe while searching for loot. By doing this you're less likely to fire off a random round attracting nearby players.

MAP MADNESS

The **complete guide** to all the locations in Fortnite Battle Royale!

D iving into Fortnite Battle Royale's map can be a little daunting at first. Where to land? Which area has the best loot? What kind of resistance are you likely to meet? There are so many variables when picking the perfect location, but don't stress it too much because we've compiled the complete guide to the map detailing every major location, plus some additional hints and tips. However, it's extremely important to remember that loot spawning locations, including weapons and Loot Chests are like a lottery and all depend on the direction of the Battle Bus approach. And, more importantly, as each season arrives Epic Games has been known to modify the map and even remove areas entirely via updates.

DUSTY DIVOT

Formerly known as Dusty Depot, Dusty Divot was completely transformed when a meteor crash-landed in the area during Season Four of Battle Royale. Gone is the industrial area that was once loaded with loot, and in its place remains a research station overrun with plant life. Dusty Divot is still a great looting spot!

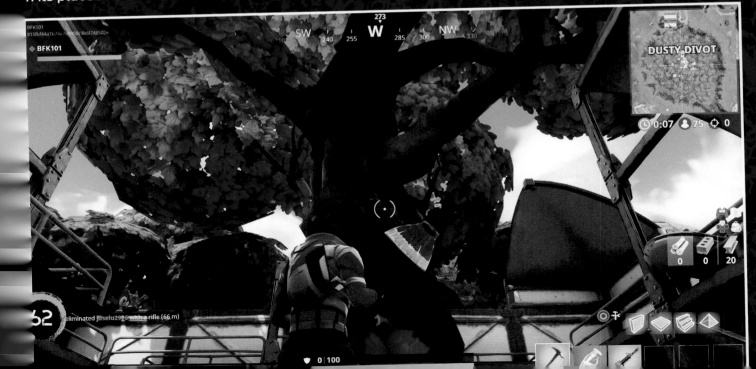

FATAL FIELDS

Fatal Fields is a large farm filled with old barns, stables, a pond and a scattering of crop fields. If you decide to drop here, be sure to take time to check each and every building for gear. There are lots of useful building materials to grab here too, including metal from vehicles and wood from the numerous buildings.

FLUSH FACTORY

Need a new toilet bowl? Head to Flush Factory, an industrial building rife with loads of building materials that can be farmed for later in the game, as well as Loot Chests. The problem with this area is that it's incredibly popular, which means you're going to face stiff competition when landing here in a match.

GREASY GROVE

Greasy Grove is a residential neighbourhood that also houses a fast food takeaway, a petrol station and an abandoned store. It's located at the southwest of the map, and while it does have a hefty helping of loot to search for, it's also quite popular amongst players. With that in mind, approach with caution.

HAUNTED HILLS

Haunted Hills is a right old spooky spot on the map. It's filled with plenty of brick to harvest, as well as multiple chests dotted around the place, including deep inside the mausoleum. However, if you do drop here you are right on the edge of the map, so when the Storm Eye starts to close in be ready to move, and fast!

JUNK JUNCTION

Junk Junction is, well, full of junk of course! That means there is a huge amount of metal to harvest here if you want to take the time to grab some while you scour the place for gear and weapons at the start of a match. Don't forget to climb high here; there can sometimes be good stuff on top of the piles of junked cars.

LAZY LINKS

Lazy Links was actually once called Anarchy Acres, but that area of the map was shelved in favour of this very stylish upgrade, which includes tennis courts, swimming pool, plush buildings, garages and a golf course. Lazy Links is great for both looting, and for finding an All Terrain Kart to drive around the map.

LONELY LODGE

Lonely Lodge has one of the best buildings to drop into at the start of a match, and that's the huge watchtower located in the area. If you can get there before anyone else you can work your way down, grabbing plenty of loot, and, if you're lucky, the odd Loot Chest. The watchtower also provides a great vantage point.

LOOT LAKE

If you are after swathes of loot then look no further than Loot Lake. This huge area houses a gargantuan lake with a house nestled in the centre of it, as well as a number of other buildings on the periphery. It's a great place for gear, but it's also very popular with players so be prepared.

LUCKY LANDING

Given it's name you'd think this Asian themed area of the Fortnite Battle Royale map would be bursting with loot and gear, but that's actually not the case. It's quite small, so if you land with other players in solo or duo modes you'd better grab a weapon quickly or risk getting taken out of the match at an early stage.

PARADISE PALMS

Replacing Moisty Mire at the outset of Season Five, Paradise Palms' biggest and coolest feature is the fact it houses a huge racetrack where you can challenge friends or other players to a race using either Shopping Carts or the All Terrain Kart. There's some good loot to be found in the buildings, but you'll need to get to it fast.

PLEASANT PARK

Located to the northwest of the map, Pleasant Park is a cosy little suburban residential area that's decked out with houses, a park and a football pitch. There are lots of looting opportunities in the houses spread out around the area, as well as in the petrol station. Just be sure to scout the area out before entering.

RETAIL ROW

This area of the map houses a huge retail complex and car park, as well as residential buildings. There are so many options for looting, so if you land here you should be able to tool-up pretty quickly. However it's a hot zone for drops, so you're going to face stiff competition when you decide to land here.

RISKY REELS

With its abandoned drive-in movie theatre, we often wonder what kind of cool flicks they used to show here before the place became part of Battle Royale. There's a huge crater in the ground after a meteor strike wrecked the place, but there are also plenty of vehicles for grabbing materials, in particular metal.

SALTY SPRINGS

Here's yet another residential area not far from Dusty Divot and Shifty Shafts that's got plenty of brick houses ideal for farming materials for battles at the end of a match, and it's pretty central too. It's also got a tower that's perfect for taking out enemies at a distance if you've got a Sniper Rifle to hand.

SHIFTY SHAFTS

Shifty Shafts is an old underground mineshaft loaded with drifts, cages and trucks, as well as incredibly tight areas that you'll have to manoeuvre around with extreme caution. With that in mind be sure to try and grab a shotgun for close encounters, because you'll last a lot longer, especially in the winding tunnels.

SNOBBY SHORES

You don't have to be snobby to drop here at the start of a match, but with its luxury houses and villas it might just help! The houses themselves are usually stacked pretty nicely with loot and building materials, so spend some time mooching throughout the area to load up before heading to the next area.

TILTED TOWERS

Tilted Towers is awesome. It's absolutely brimming with loot, as well as reams of super powerful weaponry. There are buildings galore to search through, each one with multiple floors, but if you've played the game at all you'll know that this area is without doubt the most popular drop zone for players in the game.

TOMATO TOWN

Tomato Town is quite small, and there's generally not a whole lot going on here, but if you do decide to drop into this area at the start of a match then be sure to check all the buildings, in particular the restaurant where you'll sometimes find a Loot Chest nestled behind the counter, as well as plenty of cars for metal.

WAILING WOODS

Located west of Tomato Town, Wailing Woods is a heavily forest area packed with wooden sheds that are ideal for grabbing materials, as well as a bunker and maze. It's a bit of a nightmare to manoeuvre, so take your time and be sure to seek out the shipping containers that are usually loaded with lovely loot.

OFF THE GRID

Alongside the whole host of areas we've listed, there are a handful of other locations perfect for hitting up that are absolutely rife with loot for the grabbing, and off the grid compared to Battle Royale's primary locations, which can sometimes be packed with other players and dangerous to your health. Let's take a look!

THE MOTEL

The Motel is just north of Pleasant Park right on the edge of the map. It's pretty dilapidated and is decked out with a pool, shack and decimated house. Oh, and there's a truck embedded in a part of it! It's a nifty spot to loot if you don't want to be disturbed, so be sure to check it out.

VIKING SHIP

The Viking Ship appeared at the start of Season Five, after being hinted at towards the end of Season four and is comprised of a handful of loots spots, including a Viking Ship, Fort, Longhouse and Haystack Hut. From time to time a Loot Chest appears on the Viking Ship, so be sure to keep an eye out for it.

THE MANSION

The Mansion is located on the edge of the map overlooking the ocean complete with multiple rooms, including an underground bunker that's ideal for looting in, and because it's situated so close to the ocean it's usually a good spot to drop to if you don't want to be disturbed by other players at the outset of a match.

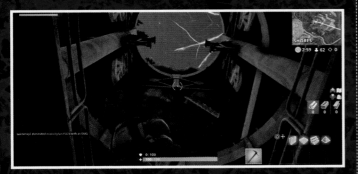

THE LAIR

Located in the mountains east of Snobby Shores the Villain Lair is shaped like a robot and filled to the brim with harvesting materials ripe for the taking, including metal, wood and brick. Hit this place up first if you're keen on grabbing mucho materials, but keep an eye out for other players with the same nefarious idea.

SHIPPING YARD

Feeling a little heavy metal? Then drop at the Shipping Yard. This place is packed to the brim with cargo containers, which means there's plenty of metal to grab for building fortifications later in the match. Besides the materials, there should be a nice supply of loot inside the containers, so be sure to search them.

SAVING THE WORLD

Wondering if you should buy **Fortnite Save The World**, if it's as much fun as Battle Royale, or how exactly the game works then read our complete guide!

What is Fortnite Save The World?

Fortnite Save The World is where it all began. The game was released in July of 2017 and is essentially a co-operative play survival game where you team up with three other players to battle waves of zombie-like enemies that will try to swarm you, destroy your buildings and generally make your life miserable. It's got pretty much all the ingredients that make the Battle Royale mode so great, including shooting and building, as well as elements of tower defence. It was created and developed by both Epic Games and People Can Fly, who crafted the awesome science fiction shooter, Bulletstorm.

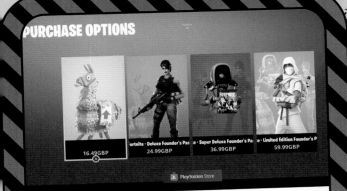

Is It Free?

Okay, let's be honest here – the biggest question you probably had was 'Is this game free?' Sadly, it's not. It costs actual money to buy. Save The World isn't too pricey though, and even though we've mentioned it a couple of times already we'll go through the different packages one more time just so you can be certain which version you're going to pick up. There are multiple versions of the game, including the Standard Edition, Deluxe Edition, Super Deluxe Edition and Limited Edition. Prices vary from platform to platform, but keep an eye out for discounts because Epic has chopped the price substantially a number of times!

I heard It Will Be Free!

Save The World will be free. It could actually be free by the time you finish reading this, but right now as we scribble this down the game is still in Early Access and we have no idea when Epic Games will push that button and make the game free for all to grab. There is a chance it could cost you nothing by the end of 2018, possibly early 2019, but right now we get the feeling the developer is incredibly focused on Battle Royale, as well as tweaking and modifying Save The World so that it's in the best possible shape before going free.

Does It Have A Story?

It does! If you like to gobble up a good tale, then you're in for a treat. 98% of the world's population has disappeared. The cause? A giant purple storm that appeared out of nowhere and now covers the entire planet. The bad news? Monsters called Husks have invaded the world, but the survivors have discovered how to build Storm Shields, which clear the strange purple clouds and reduce the number of Husk attacks. This is where you come in, taking on the role of a base leader to rescue survivors, expand the Storm Shield and smash Husks!

Can I Still Build?

Of course you can build, it wouldn't be Fortnite without building and boy does Save The World have plenty of building for you to do. The majority of your objectives throughout the huge campaign will involve building, and building big. Each of the missions require you to craft structures around machines that need to be protected from the Husk menace trying to swarm, destroy them, and whack you. Building is really easy to get to grips with, but traps also play a huge part in the game too. You'll need to lay down plenty of them to stop the beasts invading!

What Do I Do With Survivors?

As you play through the game you'll unlock survivors through Piñatas and they will appear in the rather convoluted menu system that Epic Games really needs to streamline before it makes the game free to those who haven't picked it up yet. Survivors all have different statistics and characteristics. You can then add them to your survivor squad to bolster your main characters' abilities, as well as earning other things such as tactical and support perks. If you find a Defender they'll conjure computer-controlled guards to defend your base, so be sure to utilise both of these as you play through the game.

What Are Llama Piñatas?

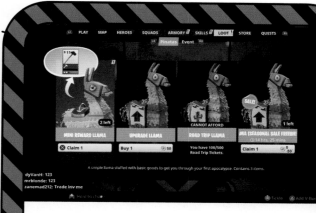

We love the Llama Piñatas. They have such a zany attitude, and constantly dole out hilarious one-liners right before you bash them to pieces to see what's inside. 'But what are they?' we hear you ask. Well, they're essentially loot boxes that can be earned by playing through the game and levelling up, or by spending real money on them. They come in different rarity styles too, and if you hit one and it turns silver you're likely to nab some good stuff. If it turns gold when smashed a second time then you are in for a treat, because there are big surprises inside.

Whoa, That Skill Tree Looks Complicated!

At first glance, yes the Skill Tree Epic Games has implemented into the game does look incredibly convoluted and complicated to a first-time player, but it's really not as tricky to manoeuvre around as you think. It just takes a little getting used to is all. There are four tiers at the top, these ones are for juicing up the different Hero Classes with each one splitting off into separate branches so that you can focus on a Hero Class of your choice. Then you have research tiers, which are used for bumping up things like a character's health. Just spend a bit of time exploring it and you'll get the hang of it quite quickly.

Can I Earn V-Bucks?

The good news is YES YOU CAN! If you've been on the fence about picking up Save The World stop procrastinating and just grab it the next chance you have. You can definitely earn V-Bucks in the game, and the best part is they are cross-transferable between it and Battle Royale mode. Of course earning V-Bucks in Save The World won't be easy. If it were everyone would be playing it and Epic Games wouldn't be one of the wealthiest game developers on the planet. To bolster your in-game bank balance you're going to have to work for it by completing Daily Quests, missions, side quests and challenges.

Stop, Stop! I Just Want To Shoot Stuff!

Calm down! Of course you shoot. In fact you'll spend just as much time blasting Husks as you will building mighty structures to keep the ghouls out. Save The World is all about the shooting, and the game, much like Battle Royale, does a damn good job of it. The difference between this and Battle Royale is that your guns degrade over time so you're going to have to either upgrade them or recycle. Guns and ammo can be crafted too, and schematics can be found in lovely Llama Piñatas so don't worry if a favoured weapon breaks down over time.

MONSTER PROBLEMS

Save the world from Fortnite's **creepy critters** determined to ruin your party!

T he primary goal in Fortnite Save The World is to build structures, protect said structures, harvest materials and complete the numerous objectives the game sets out for you. However, as you battle to do this you're faced with a problem - a monster problem involving Husks and Mist Monsters. These dastardly demons will do everything they can to smash up your buildings and kick your butt.

There is a swathe of these beasts to face off against over the course of Save The World; each one doling out attacks that range from light to extremely deadly, which means you need to know your monsters so here's a look at just some of the ghastly ghouls you'll have to face-off against in Save The World!

1 Husk

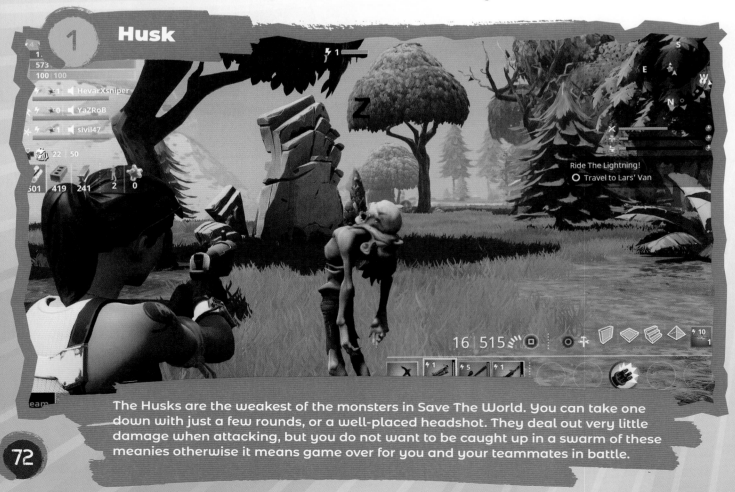

The Husks are the weakest of the monsters in Save The World. You can take one down with just a few rounds, or a well-placed headshot. They deal out very little damage when attacking, but you do not want to be caught up in a swarm of these meanies otherwise it means game over for you and your teammates in battle.

2 Husky

Husky monsters are big and bulky, and tend to be much larger than a standard Husk. They can deal out a decent amount of damage if they get too close to you or your structure, so make sure to take them down before they get within swinging distance. The best way to take them down is by hitting its big ugly head!

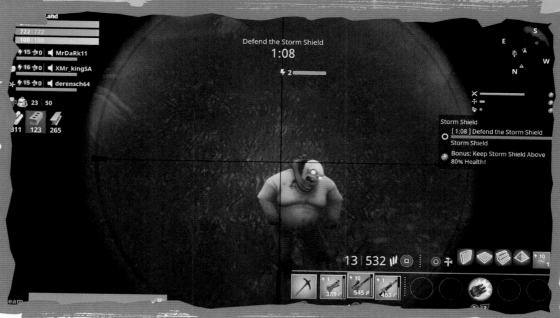

3 Pitcher

Pitchers are zany zombie-like baseball players wearing a baseball mitt filled with grimy, slimy un-dead bones that they can hurl at you from a distance, so be sure to take them down before they can sling one your way. If they do manage to get a shot off in your direction don't forget to dodge the putrid bone before it clocks you!

4 Beehive

Buzz, buzz! Beehive Husks have, um, a beehive for a head naturally! And circling around the beehive is a huge swarm of bees that they can send flying in your direction. The best way to deal with these creeps is to shoot the beehive, which turns then into normal Husks. After that, a simple headshot should do the trick!

5 Smasher

Hulk monster smash! These humongous and horrendous beasts will crash through your structures making way for other critters to pile in and decimate your squad and objectives. Be warned, these things take a lot of damage so you're going to need to either lay traps or pour every ounce of ammo you've got into 'em!

6 Shielder

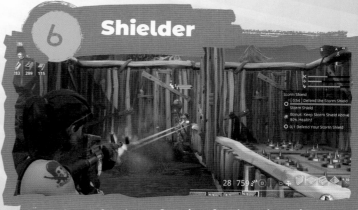

Watch out for these floating freaks when they appear on the battlefield. They're usually found hovering over another ghoul's head forming a protective purple shield around them, so take them out as quickly as possible before turning your attention to the beast it was protecting. They're not very powerful at all, so it shouldn't take much to wipe one out with a well-placed shot.

SUPER FANS

Meet some of Fortnite's biggest fans!

Fortnite Battle Royale is crazy popular. Everyone is playing it. We went out into the world to find some fans of Epic's game to ask them what they think of the world's most popular video game, and why it's such a hit amongst gamers.

CILLIAN & LENNON LAVERY

We like playing with our friends so that we can work together to get kills and wins. The game updates are really great, because they add new weapons and limited time modes. There are things that we don't like, especially lag and coming second to no-skin players. We also spend a lot of time watching YouTubers to learn new tactics, and even though the game is free we save our pocket money to buy the Battle Pass, tears, skins and dances.

SHANE DONNELLY

I absolutely love playing Fortnite Battle Royale. It's an extremely fast-paced shooter where anything can happen at a moment's notice. That and the fact it's also a strategically challenging building game, which I think is what really sets it apart from the other Battle Royale games out there. You really have to think fast or you're in deep trouble, especially later in a match when the player counter shrinks and it's just you and a handful of other players fighting.

ZACH HUMSTON

The biggest enjoyment I get out of playing the game is that I get to hang out online with my buddies. I'm playing the game on an Xbox One S, and I think it looks amazing; it's probably one of the best looking games I've ever played. There are so many weapons to pick up during a match, which means you never get bored. I also buy a lot of skins and enjoy mixing and matching, but the best feeling of all is getting that Victory Royale!

SARAH O'CONNOR

I really love playing Battle Royale, because it's such an easy game to get to grips with. There is no messing around. You just drop in and start playing, and that's what makes it so accessible. One of the things I like is the way you can choose what type of match you want to play, whether it's Solo, Duo, Squad or the 50v50, which is my favourite one to play because I feel I have a better chance at getting a Victory Royale.

AARON & DYLAN WEBB

Fortnite Battle Royale is a great game, because it's fun, exciting and sometimes it's a great way to talk to your friends outside of school. We've been playing the game between us for about nine months, and we absolutely love it! We love the weekly updates and fun challenges that Epic bring out, and we think we're pretty good at it because we practice a lot on it, but if there's one thing we don't like it's losing!

LUKE HIGGINS

I'm playing the game on PlayStation 4, and I enjoy it so much because I can play with all my mates. To be honest I don't buy a lot of skins but I do buy the battle pass when it comes out, but of the skins I do have my favourite is Whiplash because not many people use it. I haven't played Save The World yet, but I would like to try it out someday, and I hope Epic Games keep adding great stuff to the game.

LILLY O'CONNOR DONEGAN

I really enjoy playing Fortnite Battle Royale, because they have very funny dances in the game. My favourite one is The Floss; it makes me laugh so much. I also like it because it's such a fun game to play with my friends, as well as my mum who is also a big fan of the game. We play the game on the Xbox One together, which is really great to be able to do, but I'm only allowed to play a little at a time.

BARRY DUNNE

I play Fortnite on my PlayStation, and really like it being able to play with my mates. When the game first came out I played for two to three hours a day most days, but nowadays I'm just playing an hour a day, because it's so easy to get sucked into it. If there's one thing I'd like Epic to do it's introduce a mode were you can create your own private sessions to play matches with just your friends.

Go **wild** in the awesome Playground mode in Fortnite Battle Royale!

There have been a number of Limited Time Modes in Epic's monstrous multiplayer creation since its inception back in 2017, but none of them have been as eagerly anticipated as Playground, which first arrived in June 2018, before being pulled less than two hours later due to technical issues.

It returned shortly after for the duration of Season 4, before disappearing until Season 5 had gotten underway. This process is likely to continue as Epic continues to improve it with updates, but one thing is for certain – Playground mode is something we will be seeing a lot more of as Fortnite Battle Royale continues to grow and develop over the years, because it is so much fun to mess around in!

5 THINGS TO DO IN PLAYGROUND MODE

1 Target Practice

Is your aim a little shaky? Are you comfortable with some weapons and not with others? Then use Playground Mode to seek out guns and ammo, and practice hitting targets, including moving squad mates, or static targets at a distance using the Sniper Rifle. Heck, you can even build your own targets if you want

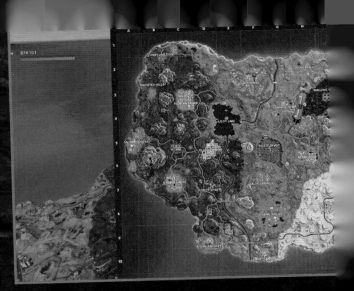

2 Build, Build, Build!

Playground Mode is the best place to practice building skills, because you will have loads of time to hone your abilities without being disturbed by other players. Besides learning the ropes in terms of basic structures, it's great for mastering the art of speed building, which will come in useful during hectic moments.

3 Master The Map

Another great thing to do is to spend time exploring every nook and cranny o the map during your time in Playground Mode. Drop in, pick a spot to land and scout out the surrounding areas, before moving onto the next area. Repeat this process until you've checked out every single area of the sprawling world.

4 Stunts

Performing cool stunts in Fortnite Battle Royale is a lot of fun, but they can be hard to do if you're in the middle of a match because you're extremely exposed while driving around in an ATK or Shopping Cart, but in Playground Mode you've got lots of time to build ramps and leap over gaping ravines!

5 Wreck Everything!

Have you ever just wanted to destroy everything? In Playground Mode you can do just that. Drop in somewhere, ready up your harvesting tool and simply smash your way to glory as you bash everything from buildings to trees to vehicles and anything else you come across before the timer runs out and the Storm arrives.

SUPER SWAG!

Awesome Fortnite merchandise every fan of the game needs in their life!

TOYS

Epic Games has teamed with Funko and McFarlane Toys to bring a collection of figurines based on characters from the game just in time for Christmas! **Get 'em!**

T-SHIRT

Proclaim your love for Fortnite everywhere you go with this **snazzy** looking T-Shirt guaranteed to turn your friends green with envy.

BASEBALL CAP

Watch people's jaws hit the floor when they see you strolling about town with this **slick** and **stylish** looking baseball cap!

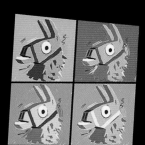

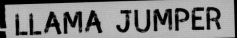

PHONE STAND

Keep dropping your phone? Don't worry, because Fortnite has got you covered with this **nifty** little Battle Bus PopSocket phone grip!

LLAMA JUMPER

Proclaim your **Llama Love** for those zany and bug-eyed Fortnite loot-containers by wearing this crazily coloured officially licensed jumper!